1 MONTH OF
FREE
READING

at
www.ForgottenBooks.com

By purchasing this book you are eligible for one month membership to ForgottenBooks.com, giving you unlimited access to our entire collection of over 1,000,000 titles via our web site and mobile apps.

To claim your free month visit:
www.forgottenbooks.com/free918696

ISBN 978-0-266-97941-8
PIBN 10918696

4—   do   do   do   do

Mortfontaine was the favourite Residence of the Ex-King and is known to many Americans as the place where the Treaty with the United States was signed.

5—Ditto

6—Ditto

7—Boguet. *Passage of the Po near Plaisance by the French Army under the command of General Bonaparte.*

The groups of Horses and Soldiers are admirable for the Details and Execution.

It was No. 107 of the Catalogue in 1845

8—Rubens & Snyders. The centre of this Picture represents the Infant Saviour and St. John and three Angels playing with a Lamb, at each side is a Pyramid of Fruits and Vegetables formed round the trunks of two Trees. Over the group of Children is a large wreath of Fruits and Flowers, with Birds on it. The figures of exquisite beauty and colouring are by Rubens and the Fruits, Birds, &c. by Snyders.

These two famous Masters frequently work-

Fourth—King of Spain.

The Dog is represented pointing at a large Hare, it is full of life and the foliage is beautifully finished.

10 to 19—Ten beautiful Engravings, framed

20—Marble Bust of Louis Bonaparte, brother of Napoleon, by Bartolini.

21—Marble Bust of Jerome Bonaparte, brother of Napoleon, by Bartolini.

22— do do of Prince Bacciochi, husband of Princess Eliza, sister to Napoleon, by Bartolini.

23—Marble Bust of Prince Borghese, husband of Princess Pauline, sister to Napoleon, by Bartolini.

24 to 27—Framed Engravings and Lithographs, representing Battles of Napoleon.

28.—LAWRENCE. *View of the old Mansion, the Park, and the Delawere River*, beautifully painted for the late Prince, by Lawrence.

29—small Marble Bust of the young Princess Camerata, daughter of Eliza, by Canova.

30—GASPAR POUSSIN. Rich Landscape, canvas 2 feet 8 inches by 2 feet 1 inch (No. 29 of 1845 sale.)

31—Framed Engraving. Serment du Jeu de Paume.

32— do do Crowning of Napoleon.

33— do do Napoleon in Imperial Robes.

34— do do Joseph, King of Spain.

35— do do Lucien as Senator.

36—BASSANO. *The Entrance into the Ark.*

The Animals in pairs, passing the foreground ; a White Horse carrying a Sack, the centre of the Group. Canvass, length 6 feet 9 inches, height 3 feet 7 inches, (No. 53 of 1845 sale.)

37—small Landscape.

38— do. do.

39—ANTONIO TEMPESTA. Battle Piece.

wife of Napoleon, by Bozio.

43—1 marble Bust of Catherine, Princess of Wirtemberg, wife of Jerome Bonaparte. By Bozio.

44—RAPHAEL MOENGS. *Nativity of our Saviour.*

This magnificient Chef d'œuvre was executed by the artist for a Monarch of Spain, as an Altar Piece, and cost an immense price. It represents the Virgin with our Saviour, and Shepherds in adoration.— Angels descending as Messengers from Heaven.

It would be useless to attempt a description of such a Painting, no pen could give an idea of its merits. The late owner with a view to encourage the Fine Arts in this country, lent it for some time to the National Academies of New York and Philadelphia, where a great number of copies were made by young Artists, who profited by his Benevolence. Canvass, length 4 feet 6 inches, height 9 feet 6 inches.

The Group of Children and the Lions were also lent to the same Acedemies.

45—View of the Park of Mortfontaine, by Bidault.

46— do. do. do. do.

47—*Napoleon in his Cabinet.* Repetition of the Painting by Rob't Lefevre.

48—RUBENS. *Two Lions and a Fawn. Episode of Paradise.*

This Painting was the No. 14 of 1845 Sale. A well known Gentleman and Amateur, Mr. F ✱ ✱ ✱ ✱ ✱ of New York, offered $2,200 for it, but the owner would not part with it at that price.

49—FRANCIS FRANK. *A Dutch Fair. Historical Painting.*

The Names of the principal Personages represented in it, might be ascertained from the Banner and Coat of Arms of

50—Landscape.

51—TENIERS. *The Elder.* Large Landscape. Card players in the foreground.

52— do. do. Figures and Cattle

These two Paintings were Nos. 103 and 104 in 1845 Sale.

Also.

A large collection of Valuable Books, bound and unbound, Reviews, Maps, Drawings, Aquarelles, Engravings, Lithographs, framed and not framed, too extensive to be enumerated in this Catalogue.

BILLIARD ROOM.

53—1 mahogany Dining Table on turned legs.

54—8 ditto Chairs, with figured hair-cloth seats.

55—1 long ditto Sofa, 12 feet in length, with large hair cushion, stuffed back and ends, covered with green figured worsted, and 2 Pillows.

56—1 ditto ditto Sofa, 9 feet in length, on turned legs with hair cushion, stuffed back and ends, covered as the above.

57—1 mahogany Pier Table, on pillars, with Italian marble top.

58—1 ditto Recess Table, with drawers, on pillars, with Italian marble top.

59—1 ditto ditto do   do   do

60—1 ditto Candle Stand.

61—1 ditto revolving-top Breakfast Table.

62—4 embroidered white muslin Curtains, with green embroidered borders, with ornaments, gilt poles and rings for two windows.

63—Ingrain Carpet, red and white figure, 80 yards.

64—1 Billiard Table, with a large supply of cues, maces and balls.

65—4 suspending brass Lamps, 3 Burners, each with chain.

66—1 ditto bronze Lamp, 3 Burners with chain and cut glass shades.

67—2 bronze Girandoles, 3 lights each, with brackets and gilt bands.

68—2 bronze and gilt Mechanical Lamps, with plain globe shades.

———

LARGE DRAWING ROOM.

69—10 very superior mahogany Chairs, with

and backs, similar covered.

72—1 ditto mahogany Sofa, to correspond, with hair cushion, ends and back, and two Pillows, similar covered.

73—2 second sized Sofas to correspond, and similar covered.

74—1 very rich mahogany Centre Table, with rich black marble top.

75—1 do do do with grey marble top.

76—1 very handsome mahogany Side Table, with grey marble top and gilt ornaments, (from the Palace of the ex-king in France.)

77—1 Pier Glass, (single plate,) in gilt frame inches by inches.

78—1 do do do inches by inches.

79—1 Fire Screen, with embroidered needle-work.

80—2 bronze and gilt Candelabras, 3 lights each, supported by cupids on pedestals.

81—2 gilt high Candlesticks.

and expensive works of art, from the palace of the Luxembourg.

83—1 magnificent bronze Urania, with sphere and time-piece, stand of two kinds of porphyry, the red and grey, very costly, from the same palace.

84—10 embroidered white muslin Curtains, with blue embossed border and drapery, fringe, tassels, gilt poles, &c., for five windows, at, per window.

85—1 royal gobelin medallion figured Carpet, (in one piece,) 22 feet 6 inches, by 29 feet 4 inches, from the same palace.

SMALL ROOM.

(Between the large Drawing Room and Library.)

86—Ingrain Carpet, 16 yards.

87—white dimity Window Curtains, with Persian drapery.

LIBRARY.

88—1 mahogany Side Table, on pillars, with grey marble top.

89—1·   do   do   do   do

90—1 mahogany Pier Table, on pillars, with grey marble top.

91—2 mahogany Lyre front Card Tables.

92—6   do   Chairs, with plain hair cloth seats.

93—1 solid mahogany Bookcase, 20 feet by 8 feet 10 inches, with 42 compartments (very valuable.)

94—Ingrain Carpet, 38 yards.

95—1 Pier Glass, in gilt frame.

96—white dimity Curtains, with Persian drapery, for 2 windows.

SMALL ANTE-ROOM.

(Between the Library and Bust Room.)

97—white dimity Window Curtain, with silk drapery.

98—Suspending bronze Lamp, with chain and cut globe shade.

99—Ingrain Carpet, 18 yards.

BUST ROOM.

100—1 mahogany Pier Table, on columns, with grey marble Top.

101—1 mahogany Tea Table, with drawer, on reeded legs.

102— 1 mahogany Tea Table, with drawer, on pillar and claw feet.

103—6 mahogany Chairs, plain hair cloth seats.

104—1 mahogany Sofa, hair cloth

105—white muslin Curtains, with yellow silk drapery and fringe, for 2 windows.

106—Ingrain Carpet, 35 yards.

107—1 Pier Glass, (single plate) in white and gilt frame.

SMALL ROOM.

(Between the Bust Room and Dining Room.)

108—Ingrain Carpet, 16 yards.

109—white muslin Window Curtain, with yel low silk drapery.

110—1 mahogany Side Table, on columns, with gray marble top.

DINING ROOM.

111—1 very rich mahogany Side Table, supported

on Egyptian columns, with black marble top and heavy gilt ornaments, (from France.)

112—1 do do do do.

113—1 mahogany Sideboard, with two drawers and folding-doors, end and back rails.

114—1   do   do   do   do

115—1   do   do with 3 drawers and 3 cupboards.

116—12   do Chairs, plain hair-cloth seats.

117—1 large mahogany Dining Table on twisted legs, with 7 leaves, (dines about 24 persons.)

118—4 large and very expensive gilt Candelabras, of 7 lights each, (from France.)

119—2 gilt mechanical Dining Lamps.

120—8 blue worsted damask Curtains, with gilt poles and ornaments for 4 windows, at, per window.

121—Brussels Carpet, 120 yards.

122—1 large white marble Tub.

HALL.

123—1 mahogany Table.

124—1   do   do

125—6 fancy painted Windsor Chairs.

126—Oil Cloth, 30 square yards.

HALL STAIRCASE.

127—Oil Cloth, (by lot) about 30 yards.

MAIN STAIRS.

128—red Venetian Carpet, on the 2nd. Stairs and Landings, 50 yards.

SECOND STORY—BATH ROOM.

129—Ingrain Carpet, 20 yards.

130—Bathing Tub.

131—Pier glass, in gilt frame.

132—white muslin Window Curtain, with drapery

STUDY.

133—1 large mahogany Book-case, with glazed doors, (extending entirely across the room.)

134—1 mahogany Paper Case, or Etagere, with 11 shelves.

135—1 do do (larger.)

136—1 do Book Case, with 6 shelves.

137—1 large mahogany Couch, with hair seat

and cushion covered with blue merino, and 2 Pillows.

138—1 mahogany Table, green Cloth Cover.

139—1   ditto   ditto, with drawer.

140—1   ditto   ditto   ditto.

141—4 Window Curtains to correspond with the Dining Room, rings, poles, &c., for 2 windows, at, per window.

142—Brussels Carpet, about 80 yards.

143—4 fancy rush seat Chairs.

THE LATE COUNT'S BED ROOM.

144—mahogany French Bedstead, with gilt ornaments and canopy top, blue worsted damask curtains, fringe and drapery.

145—Feather Bed, Bolster and Pillow.

146—3 Hair Mattresses.

147—mahogany Night Table.

148—1 very rich mahogany Escritoire, with gilt ornaments.

149—maple Bookcase, with curtains in front.

153—6 fancy rush seat Chairs.

154—black and white marble mantel Clock.

155—Mantel Glass.

156—6 red worsted Curtains, with blue drapery for 3 windows, at, per window.

157—Gobelin Carpet, (single piece,) 21 feet by 21 feet, as 49 square yards, (from Luxembourg.)

158—mahogany Fire Screen, embroidered.

TOILET ROOM.

(Adjoining the Count's Bedroom.)

159—mahogany Washstand, with white marble top.

160—Dressing Bureau, with swing glass.

161—mahogany commode Bureau.

162—Ingrain Carpet, 33 yards.

GALLERY.

163—2 large mahogany Book-cases, (between the windows.)

164—1 ditto ditto Couch, with hair cushion seat and back, covered with green merino.

165—1 ditto ditto ditto covered with blue merino.

171—2 mahogany Tables.

LARGE NORTH BED ROOM.

172—mahogany Sofa, covered with blue damask.

173— ditto French Bedstead, with canopy top and white muslin curtains.

174—Feather Bed, Bolster and Pillows.

175—3 hair Mattresses.

176—mahogany Wardrobe.

177—2 do Bureaus, with white marble tops.

178—1 do Arm Chair, with merino cover.

179—1 mahogany Fire Screen, embroidered.

180—1 do Table.

181—2 do Candle Stands.

182—6 fancy rush seat Chairs.

183—mahogany dressing Bureau.

184—1 do Night Table.

TOILET ROOM, ADJOINING.

185—2 mahogany Bureaus.

186—1 do Wash Stand.

SMALL ROOM.
(*Near the Stairs.*)

187—maple field Bedstead, with yellow nankin curtains.

188—2 hair Mattresses, Bolster and Pillow.

189—mahogany Night Table, with marble top.

190—1 small mahogany Table.

191—2 rush Chairs.

192—1 mahogany Wash Stand.

193—1 do Bureau Commode.

194—1 Candle Stand.

HALL ON THIRD STORY.

195—Oil Cloth, yards.

196—Venetian Carpet.

NORTH BED ROOM.—No. 1.

197—maple field Bedstead.

198—3 hair Mattresses, Bolster and Pillow.

199—2 mahogany Bureaus.

200—1 ditto Table.

201—1 Mantel Glass.

202—4 fancy rush seat Chairs.

203—Brussels Carpet, 60 yards.

204—white muslin Curtains for 3 windows, at, per window.

205—1 mahogany Sofa, covered with hair-cloth.

209—Mantel Glass.

210—Ingrain Carpet, 13 yards, between Rooms, No. 2, and 3.

ROOM, No. 4.—THIRD STORY.

211—Ingrain Carpet, 30 yards.

ROOM, No. 5.—THIRD STORY.

212—mahogany high-post Bedstead, with dimity curtains.

213—3 hair Mattresses, Bolster and Pillow.

214—2 mahogany Bureaus.

215—1   do   Table, on twisted legs.

216—1   do   Fire Screen.

217—1   do   Washstand.

218—1   do   Escritoire.

219—Mantel Glass, in gilt frame.

220—Ingrain Carpet, 60 yards.

221—white muslin Curtains, for 4 windows, at, per window.

222—6 fancy rush seat Chairs.

ROOM, No. 6.—THIRD STORY.

223—Ingrain Carpet, 30 yards.

224—painted Bookcase.

CHINA.

A—A beautiful Dessert Set for 18 persons, imported from England in 1838, by the late Prince—all complete. Pattern, green grouned with roses.

B—Several large dessert pieces of white French and gilt China Fruit Baskets, Ice-cream Vases, &c.

C—The balance of a white French and gilt China Set, with the letter J. Will be sold in lots or altogether to suit purchasers.

The balance of the Carpets and of the Bedding, Mattresses, Pillows, Blankets, Counterpanes, &c. &c., will be sold in Lots, numbered and assorted.

KITCHEN.

All the kitchen utensils, consisting of brass, iron, copper and tin, besides various articles not enumerated in this catalogue, will be arranged in suitable Lots previous to the sale.

CPSIA information can be obtained
at www.ICGtesting.com
Printed in the USA
BVHW041425241218
536331BV00015B/609/P